Sweets & Treats

Dessert Poems

COMPILED BY Bobbye S. Goldstein

ILLUSTRATED BY Kathy Couri

Hyperion Books for Children

NEW YORK

The text for this book is set in 18-point Berkeley.
The artwork for each picture was prepared using watercolor pencil and watercolor.

First Edition
1 3 5 7 9 10 8 6 4 2

Library of Congress Cataloging-in-Publication Data

Sweets & treats: dessert poems / [compiled] by Bobbye S. Goldstein; illustrated by
Kathy Couri.
p.   cm.
Summary: A collection of poems about desserts by children's book writers.
ISBN 0-7868-1280-X (pbk.)—ISBN 0-7868-2354-2 (lib. bdg.)
1. Desserts—Juvenile poetry. 2. Children's poetry, American. [1. Desserts—Poetry.
2. American poetry—Collections.]
I. Goldstein, Bobbye S. II. Couri, Kathy A., ill.
PS595.D46S94   1998
811'.54080355—dc21   97-34391

For our dear friends
Carolynn and Jack Prelutsky,
with whom my
husband, Gabe, and I have shared
many delightful Sweets and Treats
—B. S. G.

For my mom,
who taught me that you can't
ever have too much cake,
I love you
—K. C.

Contents

Cookies, Candy, and Cake 22

Snack Attack 32

Sweets
&
Treats

Dessert Poems

Top It Off with Fruit

Berries on the Bushes

Berries on the bushes
In the summer sun.
Bring along a bucket
And pluck every one.

Look at my teeth,
They're raspberry red.
Look at my fingers,
They're strawberry pink.
Look at my mouth,
It's huckleberry purple.
Look at my tongue,
It's blackberry ink.

EVE MERRIAM

Beneath a Blue Umbrella

Beneath a blue umbrella
a melon seller sat,
selling yellow melons,
succulent and fat.

A huge and hungry hippo
made the melon seller mad
when he swallowed all the melons
that the melon seller had.

JACK PRELUTSKY

Decisions, Decisions

What kind of dessert
Would you take
If you didn't like candy
And you didn't like cake?

How about grapefruit
Tart or sweet
It's a nutritious
Juicy treat!

CECILY MOPSEY

Forty Performing Bananas

We're forty performing bananas,
in bright yellow slippery skins,
our features are rather appealing,
though we've neither shoulders nor chins,
we cha-cha, fandango, and tango,
we kick and we skip and we hop,
while half of us belt out a ballad
the rest of us spin like a top.

We're forty performing bananas,
we mambo, we samba, we waltz,
we dangle and swing from the ceiling,
then turn very slick somersaults,
people drive here in bunches
        to see us,
our splits earn us worldly
        renown,
we're forty performing
        bananas,
come see us when
        you are in town.

JACK PRELUTSKY

The Scoop

Chocolate

Chocolate
vanilla
coffee
and peach.
Let me have a cone of each.
When I am through
I will have some more.
Then I will fall down on the floor.

KARLA KUSKIN

10

Mickey Jones

When Mickey Jones
Eats ice-cream cones
He gets himself so sticky,

It's never known
Which one is cone
And which is only Mickey.

X. J. KENNEDY

Ice Cream

Be it cone
Or be it stick
It's always
A delicious lick!

Be it cup
Or be it dish
What flavor
Is it
That you wish?

Peach, vanilla
Honeydew
Which one is
The one for you?

But be careful
Don't let it drop
Or else I'll have
To get the mop!

CARY CROCKIN

On a Trip Through Yellowstone

On a trip through Yellowstone,
Desmond held his ice-cream cone
Out for grizzly bears to savor.

Desmond's now their favorite flavor.

X. J. KENNEDY

Ice-Cream Stop

The circus train made an ice-cream stop
At the fifty-two flavor ice-cream stand.
The animals all got off the train
And walked right up to the ice-cream man.
"I'll take Vanilla," yelled the gorilla.
"I'll take Chocolate," shouted the ocelot.
  "I'll take the Strawberry," chirped the canary.
    "Rocky Road," croaked the toad.
      "Lemon and Lime," growled the lion.
    Said the ice-cream man, "'Til I see a dime,
  You'll get no ice cream of mine."
Then the animals snarled and screeched
    and growled
And whinnied and whimpered and hooted
    and howled
And gobbled up the whole ice-cream stand,
All fifty-two flavors
(Fifty-*three* with Ice-Cream Man).

SHEL SILVERSTEIN

15

Menu

My mommy goes for veggies,
my daddy goes for meat,
I go to the ice-cream store
across the street.

My mommy cuts up carrots,
my daddy chews a chop,
I make myself a sugar cone
and lick the top.

My mommy crunches celery,
my daddy dices lamb
I look in the mirror
and see how sweet I am.

EVE MERRIAM

The Ice-Cream Pain

Where the back of my throat meets the
    bottom of my brain
Comes the incredible ice-cream pain.
When I swallow wrong with a bite of
    ice cream,
It hurts so bad that I almost scream.
It freezes so bad that I want to howl
Or drink boiling water or eat a towel.
Beware of ice cream! It could drive you
    insane—
With that (Oooh! Owww!) incredible
    ice-cream pain!

JEFF MOSS

I Did Not Eat Your Ice Cream

I did not eat your ice cream,
I did not swipe your socks,
I did not stuff your lunch box
with rubber bands and rocks.

I did not hide your sweater,
I did not dent your bike,
it must have been my sister,
we look a lot alike.

JACK PRELUTSKY

The Milk-Shake Café

I went into the milk-shake café
And saw the milk-shake cows,
They stood behind the counter
In different-flavored rows.

The banana-flavored milk-shake cow
Ate bananas by the bunch,
The raspberry-flavored milk-shake cow
Had raspberries for lunch.

The lemon-flavored milk-shake cow
Sulked and spat out pips,
The orange-flavored milk-shake cow
Had orange-colored lips

To get the milk shakes frothy
There was a strange machine
That shook the mooing cows
And turned their milk to cream.

There were so many different flavors
We were spoilt for a choice,
Until one day the owner said
In a trembly sort of voice,

"Quick! Clear out of the café
I've just been told today,
The place is being raided
By the RSPCA."

BRIAN PATTEN

21

Cookies, Candy, and Cake

My Brother's Really Stingy

My brother's really stingy,
he's the lowest, he's the worst.
He never shares his lollipops
unless he licks them first.

JACK PRELUTSKY

Trifles

*Trifles
  and
    Truffles
      are
        easy
          to
            eat
              Delicious
                Delightful
                  Delectable
                    Treats!

*A trifle is an English treat
It's tasty and it's very sweet
It's made with cake and jam and cream
So fattening it could split a seam!

FREDERIC S. GOLDSTEIN
BOBBYE S. GOLDSTEIN

Someone Swiped the Cookies

Someone swiped the cookies
that were really meant for me.
I'm sure I know who did it,
she'll regret her little spree.
She snuck into the pantry
where she found the cookie jar,
she thinks she's really clever,
but she won't get very far.

I'm tracking down the culprit,
she should not be hard to find.
She left a very messy trail
of cookie crumbs behind.
There she is! I've got her!
She has crumbs around her lips!
Oh no! She finished every one . . .
my luscious chocolate chips.

JACK PRELUTSKY

Grandma Louise's Gingerbread

Grandmama made gingerbread—
her writing's on this card—
her recipe in curled black script
directs, "Don't beat too hard."

My mother ate it after school
cut in a warm brown square
when she was just a little girl,
and Grandmama was there.

Sugar, egg, and buttermilk,
molasses, ginger, flour—
mix and measure, put to bake
only half an hour.

I never met my grandmama
and never will (she's dead),
but I kind of know her, since
I eat her gingerbread.

CRESCENT DRAGONWAGON

A Moon in Your Lunch Box

There's a moon
in your lunch box—
I'm not kidding.

Someone left it
like an extra cookie
on a plate of sky,
and I
snatched it up
this morning
just for you.

It was cool
to the touch
and slightly rough,
and I put it there
between your apple
and your sandwich,
glowing.

Take a look,
but don't show
the others—

it's a secret moon
inside your lunch box,

and it is
just for you.

MICHAEL SPOONER

31

Snack Attack

The Snack Attack

When you have a snack attack
What's the way that you fight back?
Peanuts, pretzels, potato chips,
Which will make you smack
    your lips?
Neither, neither will it be,
Chocolate is the choice for me!

BOBBYE S. GOLDSTEIN

Pop, Pop, Popcorn

When you have nothing to do
Pop some popcorn just for you
See the little kernels pop
Keep on watching till they stop
If they pop into the air
They might land up in your hair
If they fall down on the floor
Then you'll have to make some more
And the best is yet to come
As you end up eating some!

CECILY MOPSEY

Chocolate-Covered Salami

Chocolate-covered salami,
Broccoli chocolate fudge,
Spinach in chocolate syrup,
Chocolate sauerkraut sludge.

Pickles in chocolate pudding,
Chocolate fish fricassee—
If it has chocolate on it,
Then it is a snack made for me.

JACK PRELUTSKY

Enjoy More Hyperion Chapter Books!

ALISON'S PUPPY

SPY IN THE SKY

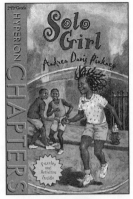

SOLO GIRL

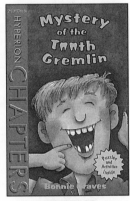

**MYSTERY OF
THE TOOTH GREMLIN**

**MY SISTER
THE SAUSAGE ROLL**

I HATE MY BEST FRIEND

**ALISON'S FIERCE AND
UGLY HALLOWEEN**

SECONDHAND STAR

GRACE THE PIRATE

Hyperion Chapters

2nd Grade
Alison's Fierce and Ugly Halloween
Alison's Puppy
Alison's Wings
The Banana Split from Outer Space
Edwin and Emily
Emily at School
The Peanut Butter Gang
Scaredy Dog
Sweets & Treats: Dessert Poems

2nd/3rd Grade
The Best, Worst Day
I Hate My Best Friend
Jenius: The Amazing Guinea Pig
Jennifer, Too
The Missing Fossil Mystery
Mystery of the Tooth Gremlin
No Copycats Allowed!
No Room for Francie
Pony Trouble
Princess Josie's Pets
Secondhand Star
Solo Girl
Spoiled Rotten

3rd Grade
Behind the Couch
Christopher Davis's Best Year Yet
Eat!
Grace the Pirate
The Kwanzaa Contest
The Lighthouse Mermaid
Mamá's Birthday Surprise
My Sister the Sausage Roll
Racetrack Robbery
Spy in the Sky
Third Grade Bullies